WILD WEST LEGENDS

Elizabeth Raum

Raintree

Chicago, Illinois

Designed by Victoria Bevan, Steve Mead,
and Bigtop
Printed and bound in China by Leo Paper Group

12 11 10 09 08
10 9 8 7 6 5 4 3 2 1

**Library of Congress
Cataloging-in-Publication Data**
Raum, Elizabeth.
 Wild west legends / Elizabeth Raum.
 p. cm. -- (Atomic)
 Includes bibliographical references and index.
 ISBN 978-1-4109-2968-6 (library binding -
hardcover) -- ISBN 978-1-4109-2989-1 (pbk.)
 1. Pioneers--West (U.S.)--Biography--Juvenile
literature. 2. Cowboys--West (U.S.)--Biography-
-Juvenile literature. 3. Outlaws--West (U.S.)--
Biography--Juvenile literature. 4. Frontier and
pioneer life--West (U.S.)--Juvenile literature.
5. West (U.S.)--Biography--Juvenile literature.
6. West (U.S.)--History--1860-1890--Juvenile
literature. I. Title.

 F594.R285 2007
 978--dc22
                              2006100829

Acknowledgments
The author and publisher are grateful to the
following for permission to reproduce copyright
material: AKG-images p. **14** bottom; Buffalo
Bill Historical Center p. **7**; Corbis pp. **14** top, **21**
bottom, **5** bottom; Corbis/Bettmann pp. **5** top, **6**, **9**,
10 (Philip Gendreau), **13**, **16**, **18**, **19**, **21** top, **25**,
26; Getty Images/Hulton Archive/D. F. Barry p. **22**.

Cover photograph of Buffalo Bill reproduced with
permission of Getty Images/Hulton Archive.

Photo research by Mica Brancic
Illustrations by Jeff Edwards

The publishers would like to thank Nancy Harris,
Dee Reid, and Diana Bentley for their assistance in
the preparation of this book.

Every effort has been made to contact copyright
holders of any material reproduced in this book.
Any omissions will be rectified in subsequent
printings if notice is given to the publishers.

Contents

Jesse James 4–7

Wild Bill Hickok... 8–11

Calamity Jane.. 12–15

Billy the Kid 16–19

Buffalo Bill 20–23

Annie Oakley 24–27

A Look Back at the Legends 28–29

Glossary 30

Want To Know More? 31

Index 32

Some words are printed in bold, **like this**. You can find out what they mean in the glossary. You can also look in the box at the bottom of the page where the word first appears.

JESSE JAMES

On February 13, 1866, Jesse James and his brother Frank entered the National Bank of Liberty, Missouri. They demanded money.

Wanted!

"Be quick," they said, as the nervous bank clerk loaded gold and silver coins into a sack. The outlaws rode off with over $57,000.

Between 1866 and 1882, Jesse James stole over $200,000 from banks and trains. During the robberies, he killed **unarmed** men. The state of Missouri offered $10,000 for Jesse James, dead or alive. Bob Ford, a member of James's gang, killed him on April 3, 1882, for the reward money.

Wild West Fact!

James read three newspapers every day so that he could follow stories of his own bank robberies.

unarmed	without weapons

Jesse James was 17 years old in this photo.

People said that Jesse James robbed from the rich and was kind to the poor—but this has never been proved.

Dime novels like this turned
Jesse James into a hero.

Wild West Fact!

James wrote letters to local
newspapers claiming he was not
a robber. On August 18, 1876,
he wrote to the *Kansas City
Times*: "I can ... show ... that I
was not at the train robbery."

Dime novels said that Jesse James was "America's **Robin Hood**." But James never gave money to the poor like Robin did. He kept it for himself and his gang.

Hero or villain?

No one denies that Jesse James loved his family. He was fearless and brave. However, he was also a thief and a murderer.

Jesse James has become a **legend**. But was he a hero? What is the difference between a legend and a hero?

Jesse James loved his children, Mary and Jesse Jr.

dime novel	low-priced paperback book
legend	popular story that is hard to prove
Robin Hood	legendary English outlaw from around the 1200s who robbed from the rich to help the poor

WILD BILL HICKOK

In 1865 James Butler Hickok (known as Wild Bill) played a game of cards with Dave Tutt in Springfield, Missouri. The two argued. Later they faced one another in front of a courthouse.

Both men drew their guns, but Hickok was faster. He shot Tutt through the heart at a distance of 100 **paces**.

Trial

Hickok was arrested and put on trial. The **jury** agreed with Hickok's claim that he was defending himself, so he was released.

Hickok's fame earned him the job of **sheriff** in several Kansas towns. He often spent his time playing cards until his **deputies** alerted him to a problem.

deputy	assistant to the sheriff
jury	group of people who decide guilt or innocence in a trial
pace	step used to measure length
sheriff	person in charge of a local police force

Newspapers reported that Wild Bill Hickok was a handsome man.

Wild Bill Hickok was shot dead in a saloon by a man named Jack McCall

An 1867 magazine article described Wild Bill Hickok as a brave gunfighter who tamed the **Wild West**. Not everyone agreed. For example, Hickok was fired as sheriff of Abilene, Kansas, because he killed two men. During his years as a sheriff, he killed seven men.

Hickok the hero?

Some people call Hickok a murderer. However, others say that during a period when everyone carried guns, he helped keep down the number of killings.

Would you call Hickok a hero? Why or why not?

Wild West Fact!

Hickok usually sat with his back to a wall, so that no one could sneak up on him. On August 2, 1876, he was killed while playing cards—with his back to the door—in Deadwood, Dakota Territory.

Wild West   **Western United States before law and order**

CALAMITY JANE

Martha Jane Cannary (known as Calamity Jane) could shoot, swear, and drink like a man. In the 1870s many jobs were not open to women, so Calamity Jane dressed like a man and did men's work.

Exciting adventures

Calamity Jane said that she rode for the **Pony Express**, fought the Native Americans in 1875, and married Wild Bill Hickok, whom she met in 1876.

Yet most of Calamity Jane's stories were untrue. When she wrote her **autobiography**, she made up exciting adventure stories.

autobiography — story of one's own life

Pony Express — mail delivery service that used riders on fast horses

Calamity Jane often wore men's clothes.

Calamity Jane poses at Wild Bill Hickok's grave in Deadwood. Despite her claims, there is no proof that she and Hickok were ever married.

In 1953 a movie was made based on Calamity Jane's life. It starred Doris Day as Calamity.

Dime novels often featured the adventures of Calamity Jane. These novels—and her own stories about herself—turned her into a hero.

True or untrue?

It is not always easy to know what is true about Calamity Jane. However, we know for sure that she cared about others. A doctor from the town of Deadwood reported that Calamity Jane risked her own health to nurse the sick during a **smallpox epidemic**.

Plays, movies, and television shows continue to paint a colorful picture of Calamity Jane. Was she simply an entertaining character, or was she a hero? What do you think?

epidemic	outbreak of a deadly disease
smallpox	disease with fever and vomiting that leaves marks on the skin

BILLY THE KID

On April 28, 1881, Billy the Kid was in jail in Lincoln, New Mexico. He was charged with murder. At dinnertime, Billy asked to use the outhouse. One deputy led him outside.

Shoot to kill

On the way back, Billy knocked the deputy down the stairs, stole his gun, and killed him.

Billy ran back inside. From a second-storey window, he shot and killed the remaining deputy, who was on the street below.

Billy stepped onto the balcony and told the townspeople that he was sorry he had killed the first deputy. He was a good man. The second deputy, he said, deserved to die.

| outhouse | bathroom located in a separate building |

This is one of the few pictures of Billy the Kid.

Wild West Fact!

Billy the Kid also spoke Spanish. This made him popular with Mexicans who lived in the area.

REWARD
($5,000.00)

Reward for the capture, dead or alive, of one Wm. Wright, better known as

"BILLY THE KID"

Age, 18. Height, 5 feet, 3 inches. Weight, 125 lbs. Light hair, blue eyes and even features. He is the leader of the worst band of desperadoes the Territory has ever had to deal with. The above reward will be paid for his capture or positive proof of his death.

JIM DALTON, Sheriff.

DEAD OR ALIVE!
"BILLY THE KID"

Billy the Kid left town. Less than three months later, **Sheriff** Pat Garrett gunned him down.

Friend or enemy?

People who knew Billy found him friendly and charming. They said he was intelligent, but quick-tempered. However, newspapers of the day called him a dangerous killer.

In 1926 a book about Billy painted a different picture. It claimed that he killed and stole to help poor people. There is little proof to support this idea.

Billy the Kid fascinates us. Why is that? What draws us to characters like him?

Wild West Fact!

Some stories say that Billy the Kid killed 21 men, one for each year of his life. The true count is closer to six.

Sheriff Pat Garrett and his men finally caught and killed Billy the Kid.

BUFFALO BILL

William Cody hunted buffalo. He supplied the meat to railroad workers. As part of this job, Cody probably killed about 10,000 buffalo. This earned him the nickname Buffalo Bill.

Pony Express rider

Buffalo Bill was always adventurous. At age 14 he rode for the **Pony Express**. He set a record by carrying the U.S. mail 322 miles (518 kilometers) during a 22-hour ride. He used 21 different horses.

In 1883 at age 37, Buffalo Bill created a touring **Wild West** show. It became a popular entertainment.

Wild West Fact!

Buffalo Bill never swore. His favorite sayings were "Thunderation" and "You can bet your boots and socks."

Buffalo Bill once made the third-longest ride in Pony Express history.

Buffalo Bill's Wild West show brought the Wild West to life for people in the eastern United States and Europe.

Buffalo Bill became friends with Sitting Bull, a **Dakota Indian** chief.

Buffalo Bill Cody understood that people would pay to see Native Americans in his Wild West show. He also thought they would like to see a live buffalo onstage.

Helpful or not?

Some people think Buffalo Bill took advantage of Native Americans by putting them on display. However, others say he treated them well. At a time when many people needed jobs, he provided them for these people.

Some people consider Buffalo Bill a buffalo killer. Others say that by using a real buffalo in his shows, he helped preserve the buffalo. He did this by attracting public interest.

What do you think? Was Buffalo Bill a hero? Why or why not?

Dakota Indians   **Native American peoples from the northern plains of the United States**

Annie Oakley

Phoebe Ann Moses (later known as Annie Oakley) began hunting at age six to provide food for her family. By age 15 she made a living supplying fresh meat to a hotel near her home in Cincinnati, Ohio.

"Little Sure Shot"

The hotel owner set up a contest between Phoebe and a **sharpshooter** named Frank Butler. Phoebe won! A year later she married Butler and changed her name to Annie Oakley. Frank and Annie toured the country as sharpshooters. In 1884 Annie met Sitting Bull. He gave her the nickname "Little Sure Shot."

Wild West Fact!

In a rifle competition, Oakley hit 943 out of 1,000 glass balls that were tossed up into the air.

sharpshooter   someone who is skilled with a gun

This photo shows Oakley in 1889 wearing the medals she won in shooting contests.

Annie Oakley taught women to shoot. This was a new thing for women and girls.

In 1885 Annie Oakley joined Buffalo Bill's **Wild West** show and traveled around the world. Audiences loved her. She was a tiny woman who weighed only 100 pounds (45 kilograms). But she could outshoot any man.

Innocent or violent?

Oakley remained with the show for 16 years. In 1915 she moved to Pinehurst, North Carolina, where she taught women to shoot. The world remembers Oakley as a strong, talented woman. Her interesting life is celebrated in books, movies, and even a Broadway musical called *Annie Get Your Gun*.

Oakley was a popular entertainer. She became a **legend**. Do you consider her a hero? Why or why not?

Wild West Fact!

After a day of shooting, Oakley enjoyed needlework and embroidery.

A Look Back At The Legends

What makes these legends so interesting? Why do we still care about these legends of the Wild West?

Do you consider any of the legends to be heroes? Which ones? Why?

If you could meet one of these legends, which one would you choose? Why?

② Annie Oakley

Also known as: Phoebe Anne Moses, Mrs. Frank E. Butler

Born: 1860, Ohio

Lived in: Ohio, New Jersey, North Carolina, Florida

Died: 1926, Ohio

① Billy The Kid

Also known as: William Bonney, Henry McCarty, Henry Antrim, William Wright

Born: 1859(?), New York

Lived in: Indiana, Kansas, New Mexico, Arizona

Died: 1881, New Mexico

③ Jesse James

Also known as: Dingus (by his gang)

Born: 1847, Missouri

Lived in: Missouri

Died: 1882, Missouri

4 CALAMITY JANE

Also known as: Martha Jane Cannary

Born: 1852, Missouri

Lived in: Utah, Montana, Dakota Territory, Wyoming, Kansas

Died: 1903, Dakota Territory

5 WILD BILL HICKOK

Also known as: James Butler Hickok

Born: 1837, Illinois

Lived in: Nebraska, Kansas, Dakota Territory

Died: 1876, Dakota Territory

6 BUFFALO BILL

Also known as: William Cody

Born: 1846, Iowa

Lived in: Kansas, Nebraska, Colorado, New York, England

Died: 1917, Colorado

The numbers on this map of the United States show where the Wild West Legends lived.

Glossary

autobiography story of one's own life

Dakota Indians Native American peoples from the northern plains of the United States

deputy assistant to the sheriff. Wild Bill Hickok relied on his deputies.

dime novel low-priced paperback book

epidemic outbreak of a deadly disease

jury group of people who decide guilt or innocence in a trial

legend popular story that is hard to prove

outhouse bathroom located in a separate building

pace step used to measure length

Pony Express mail delivery service that used riders on fast horses

Robin Hood legendary English outlaw from around the 1200s who robbed from the rich to help the poor

sharpshooter someone who is skilled with a gun

sheriff person in charge of a local police force

smallpox disease with fever and vomiting that leaves marks on the skin

unarmed without weapons

Wild West Western United States before law and order

Want to Know More?

Books

✷ Harrison, Peter, and Norman Bancroft Hunt. *World of the Wild West*. New York: Southwater, 2000.

✷ Murray, Stuart. *Wild West*. New York: Dorling Kindersley, 2005.

✷ Platt, Richard. *Explorers: Pioneers Who Broke New Boundaries*. New York: Dorling Kindersley, 2001.

Websites

✷ www.bbhc.org/home/index_flash.cfm
Visit the Buffalo Bill Historical Center to learn more about Buffalo Bill and the Wild West.

✷ www.nativeamericans.com
Learn more about Native Americans.

If you liked this Atomic book, why don't you try these...?

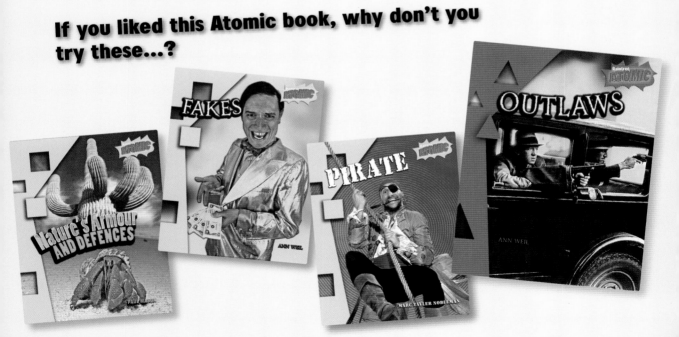

Index

autobiographies 12

bank robberies 4
Billy the Kid 16–19, 29
buffalo 20, 23
Buffalo Bill (William Cody) 20–23, 27, 29
Butler, Frank 24

Calamity Jane (Martha Jane Cannary)
    12–15, 29
card games 8, 11

deputies 8, 16
dime novels 6, 7, 15

Ford, Bob 4

Garrett, Pat 19
gunfights 8

heroes 6, 7, 11, 15, 27

James, Frank 4
James, Jesse 4–7, 28

killings 4, 11, 16, 19

legends 7, 27, 28

McCall, Jack 10
movies 14, 15, 27

Native Americans 12, 22, 23

Oakley, Annie (Phoebe Ann Moses)
    24–27, 28

Pony Express 12, 20, 21

reward money 4, 18
Robin Hood 7

sharpshooters 24
sheriffs 8, 11, 19
shooting contests 24, 25
Sitting Bull 22, 24
smallpox epidemic 15

train robberies 4, 6
Tutt, Dave 8

Wild Bill Hickok (James Butler Hickok)
    8–11, 12, 14, 29
Wild West 11
Wild West shows 20, 21, 23, 27